I Am
by B. C. Clare

ISBN: 978-1-9992111-2-7 (Paperback)
ISBN: 978-1-9992111-3-4 (Electronic Book)

Book Cover by B. C. Clare, painting by Kieran Stiles
Second edition 2022

To know thyself is the beginning of all wisdom,

and yet all I know is I know nothing.

Table of Contents

Introduction

I didn't think I would make it to thirty. When I entered my twenties, I couldn't see myself growing old. I couldn't see myself having the perseverance—or even motivation—to withstand life's throes. I couldn't see myself ever being truly happy.

Then, by some longwinded miracle, I was. By divine grace, I survived those fatal moments of sheer hopelessness. I tria-and-errored my way through depression. I started taking Vitamin D. I did yoga. I travelled. I moved cities. I found my limit and stopped pushing myself past it. I focused on mundane miracles, such as flowers just existing. I had conviction in my calling and dreams; first as a pastor and songwriter, then as a writer. I went back to school and savoured every opprtunity to learn. I soaked in the joy of creating worlds and stories and art. I found friends who didn't make me feel like a burden when I wasn't my usual, bubbly self. I fell in love with meeting new people and learning new perspectives. Then there was a two year pandemic. It was the worst two years of my life.

I lost myself—my energy, my confidence, my passion— and I've been trying to find myself ever since. If I gave a word to 2022, it would be 'Recovery'. I have not only been recovering from the pain, but I've been trying to recover who I am. Again.

In the last months of being twenty nine, in the Year of Recovery, I was forced to reckon with my own identity. I went to a writing retreat in Northern Ireland when this poetry collection started to manifest itself. I started to find my anwers to the age old question: Who am I?

I listened to Glenn Paterson read his piece entitled *I Am* and it brought me out of myself. I was inspired to write *I am a universe*, the first poem in this collection; an ode to the women who have come before me. I have been reconnecting with my ancestors for five years, researching them through online records and asking family members about them. Although I wrote this poem in one day, it took me five years to create.

Another speaker at this retreat had asked us to close our eyes and imagine a door. We were instructed to open the door, and on the other side, what we saw was ourselves.

"What do you see?" He asked.

I saw a translucent Russian doll. The vision was confusing and convoluted. The dolls looked nothing alike. Different hair colours and styles. Some wore glasses and braces. They even had different thoughts within their little, wooden heads. But they all had the same eyes.

Barry Taylor ran a session on branding and authenticity.

"Don't think about how you brand yourself," he said, "but how you want to present yourself to the world."

"I want to present myself honestly... and honestly, I'm a mess," I thought. "I am an incomprehensible image of Russian dolls trying to burst out from within their mother doll."

So when Barry said, "There is no real you. There are real *yous*," I gave a sigh of relief. I am multitudes. We all are. He continued on in brilliance:

"Through each trauma, we shed skin like snakes. We don't transform. We don't change. We just come to terms with ourselves."

That's what this project is, I suppose. I'm coming to terms with all of my snake skins and displaying them in this curiosity shop of a book. I am honouring my Russian dolls and lining them up, side by side; telling their story one by one.

I turn thirty in ten days. While most people I know struggle with this birthday—especially women—this has been my most significant birthday yet. I've made it. Not in my career or family life necessarily, but in life itself. I've made it. I am living and breathing. I am a mess, but it's extravagant and expansive.

There are thirty poems in this collection to mark the fact that this book is my thirtieth birthday gift to all of my selves. Most of the poems were written over the past few months, though I've included eight poems which were written between 2013-2021: *Black Air* (2013), *Wonderer* (2013), *A Daughter and a Sister* (2015), *The Royal Mountain* (2016), *Passerby* (2016), *Wanderer* (2016), *Dreamer* (2019), and *The Virgin and the Whore* (2021).

I've ordered the poems chronologically, according to the version of myself the poem is giving voice to.

This work has brought me peace and joy, and I hope it does the same for others as well. One of my most treasured lessons from my twenties is this:

The more I get to know others, the more I get to know myself.

So as you read this book and get to know all of me, may it inspire you in your own identity and self-understanding.

In Love,

I am a universe

I am a universe
and within me are worlds of women.

Marie Yvette Clarisse Patry.
My Mémé.
Clare had a French accent.
I remember the sad, smokey walls of her apartment.
I remember she was lonely after Pépé died.
When the matriarchs gathered, there was tension in the
          room.
I knew as a child not to speak, for the air was stale and
          fragile.

Clare was the daughter of Eva Arpin.
Eva was never in the room with us for she died in 1931
after her braids had been cut by the Catholic Priests.
Clare learned to hate her mother's braids, for what they
          meant.
"Cannibals," they whispered.
"We come from Cannibals."

I am a universe
and within me are worlds of women.

Vivian Clara Brunoe.
Vivian looked like a movie star.

That's what my grandpa told me.
She's an avid gardener now, always tending to her tomatoes and
        cannabis.
It helps with the shaking—the marijuana.
MS and Parkinson's aren't truly hereditary,
But my world still stops every time I notice my hands shaking.

Vivian ran away from her mother, Clare, at 16.
Her daughter, Susanne, did the same at 18.
Susanne's daughter ran away from her mother as well.
She ran the farthest.
But running isn't hereditary, either.

I am a universe
and within me are worlds of women.

Christine Catherine Ross.
She had a Nova Scotian accent.
Christine had no joy as a farmer's wife.
Her daughter, Jessie, grew to be 94 years old.
She repeated over and over again in her dying days,
"She hated me. My mother hated me.
Even as a little girl, she hated me.
Her name was Christine."
She wanted me to remember that.
Jessie never bore children herself, but she was a mother,
and she never stopped being a daughter.

I am a universe
and within me are worlds of women.

Mary Bohayenko.
Mary was only mentioned in whispers.
A mother who couldn't raise her children.
The ghost sister of Anne.
Anne spoke English and Ukrainian.
She took care of her sisters, all of them.
Including Mary's child, my grandpa.
Including her sister, Motria, left behind in Russia-occupied
            Ukraine.
Including Olga.
Anne was a good woman.

I am a universe
and within me are worlds of women.

Enid Price.
Enid had an upper class accent.
She was a favourite student of Stephen Leacock,
first woman to get a PhD at McGill University,
President of the National Council of Women,
Vice President of the International Council of Women.
She *travelled.*
Enid won the women's vote, not only in Canada, but around the
            world.
The silk kimono she was honoured with in Japan is way too big

　　　for me,
but I wear it anyway.

I am a universe
and within me are worlds of women.

Elizabeth Ann McDermott.
I only learned her name when I applied for my fathers original
　　　birth certificate.
"Sign the dotted line," I told him.
I found out she was eighteen when she gave birth in secret, at the
　　　edge of Newfoundland.
She hailed from Ireland,
so she already knew something of separation when she left her
　　　son at the hospital and returned home.
She doesn't know that that ginger babe of hers gave her a
　　　granddaughter who still yearns for her.
If you see her, could you let her know?

I am a universe
and within me are worlds of women.

I am the daughter of Clare, Vivian and Susanne,
the runaways.
I am the daughter of Christine and Jessie,
the scorned.
I am the daughter of Mary and Anne,
the burdened.

I am the daughter of Enid,
the accomplished.
I am the daughter of long, lost Elizabeth.

I inherited their names, their losses, their gains.
Clare's anger.
Jessie's grief.
Mary's neurosis.
Anne's devotion.
Enid's ambition.
I like to think I have Elizabeth's hair.

I am a *woman*
and within me are worlds of women.

Too Much

Children are too much for adults.
Some children are too much even for other children.

I don't stuff my face in cake anymore.
I don't wear bright colours anymore.
I don't cry when I feel like it anymore.

I love wearing lipstick,
but I always feel like it's too much.
I feel guilty when I catch myself talking about Shakespeare
        or Psychology or Theology.
"I'm sorry, I'm talking too much..." I say.
"No, this really fascinates me!" They say.
But I don't believe them.
And even if it were true,
I've talked myself into discomfort.

I hate how loud I am during sex.

When did feeling too much for others
turn into feeling too much for myself?

I úsed to make people laugh more.

Protected

Everyone knew but me.
I was twelve.
I was young,
and I was sensitive,
and I was old enough to know what the whispering meant.
I would try to get answers I didn't want.
I would sit on the green velvet sofa and just think.
I would grieve alone and in confusion.
Because I was young.
Because no one wanted to break it to me.

I was told that everything was going to be okay,
but I wasn't told what I needed to hear.
I wasn't told the truth.

My siblings knew.
My camp counsellors knew.
My friend's parents knew.
My best friends may have even known.
But they all pretended like they didn't.
They listened as I told them about how scared I was.
They listened as I told them about the nightmares I was
          having
of my parents getting divorced.
They listened and kept from me what I most needed to hear.
To spare me from the truth.

Not only did I grieve my family's fracturing,
my world falling apart,
my father cast out, my mother broken,
the grief was paired with the sting of betrayal
and humiliation
and loneliness
by being the only one who didn't know.

I was twelve
but I was sensitive
enough to feel the tension when my parents grabbed my
        hockey bag luggage,
to feel the rage in my father's voice as he finally spoke the
        truth and slammed the van door,
to feel the loneliness when I was the only one who cried on the
        way home
because everyone already knew
but me.

Protected, part 2

I was engaged.

It was complicated when
he didn't tell me
he fell in love with someone else.

He couldn't tell me, he said.
He didn't want to hurt me, he said.

I had to figure it out myself.
Again.

The worst feeling is knowing
without fully knowing.

If only people respected me
more than they protected me.

Self-titled trust fall champion

I fall and I commit.
Arms out like Jesus,
body straight like a wooden board,
my heels hinged to the floor
as I sacrifice fear for joy.

No twitch, no jerk,
no last minute stepping back.
I fall and I commit
to being caught
or thudding to the ground,
dependent upon the whim of another.

I was never good at sports,
or school, or art,
but this I was good at—
even after being dropped.

I fall and I commit,
not because I have a radical faith in my partner,
but because I like the way my heart falls into my stomach.
Because I quickly became addicted to
the shared joy of catching and being caught.

Baptised by the pen

There was no room for me at the lunch table.
No chair for me to sit in.
I knew they didn't want me there
but I grabbed a high stool
and sat awkwardly among the girls.

The boys loved to use me as a punchline,
but they were never brave enough to punch me.
Instead they played catch with a pencil case,
one of them stood behind me.
I didn't know what they were doing until the pencil case hit me
          square in the face.
Every inch of my face fell victim to the brutal impact of hard
          pencils on bone and cartilage.
My glasses and braces multiplied the damage.

Everyone waited for my reaction.

My whole body activated as if I had just been attacked.
As if I had just been attacked.
I had just been attacked.

"WHAT THE HELL?" I screamed, voice breaking.
Hell was a bad word,
but I was so angry.
I meant it.

I couldn't let them see me cry,
so I stormed out,
holding my assailed face,
and the class burst out in
uproarious laughter.

It all happened again
the very next day.

A Daughter and a Sister

A new battle begins
Armies to their lines
There's change in the wind
You've one foot on either side
The first strike was made
But you shut your eyes
You couldn't bear the pain
Two halves of you collide

Your kingdom crashing
Your eyes are to the hills
You know now inside you
It will never be as before
Your time draws near now
To trust in the Lord
Your time draws near now
To face this wretched war

I know it's breaking you
This hideous truth
Your pain is breaking through
This love it strengthens you

Stand firm

The Lord has not forsaken you

Stand tall

Though your worst fears are coming true

Draw back

And calm the raging of your heart

Aim high

Your arrow to the sky

Coxwain

The sky was starting to lighten at 5:00am.
The sight of my breath in front of me
made me feel real.
Lift to shoulder in three, two, one, *lift…*
The river's foggy breath welcomed us
as it rolled away.
Drop to waist in three, two, one, *drop…*
Before we knew it we were on the glassy water
where we belonged.
Push from deck in three, two, one, *push…*
all bundled up in my cox box.

Every morning I witnessed the world at peace,
glimpsed the secret truth that life was beautiful
before going to school and life was ugly again.
I got to peak into the magic of early mornings
and I carry that magic with me
everytime I recall the beaver,
wet and eager,
swimming alongside me
to wish me good morning.

Eunuch

The Lord said there are those who were born eunuchs from their
        mother's womb.
The Lord said there are those who have been mutilated into
        eunuchs.
The Lord said there are those who have made themselves
        eunuchs.
The Lord said "The one who can accept this should accept it."

The Lord's words sang from the page, encircling me in love:
"Holy, Holy Holy, my daughter you are found
worthy and accepted as you are.
Holy, Holy, Holy, there is freedom here;
there is more than one way to live."

"I think I'm a eunuch," I said,
and everyone laughed.

"You don't know what you're talking about," they said.
I didn't fully know what I was talking about,
but I wasn't wrong.

The word intersex did not exist.
The word asexual did not exist.
The word transgender did not exist.
But there was a word that existed
outside the gender binary,

outside the patriarchal, heteronormative script,
and two thousand years ago
I would have been a eunuch,
and I would have been accepted,
baptised on the road to Gaza,
singing, "Holy, Holy, Holy,
there is freedom here.
Hallelujah,
this is the good news."

Wonderer

you're a tired mind
gets lost sometimes
in thoughts and questions seem to gather
together in unity
trying to throw you off your feet
when your mind starts getting deep
you stop and ask what's even the matter
what's it all matter?

and there's a bird alone on the pier
he's not afraid to get near to you
and you feel the water splashing on your shoes as he winces his
          eyes looking for something new
the wind is so strong blowing away his feathers he can barely
          stand and now I'm
watching the seagull make its flight from land
and instead of letting the wind wisk him away
he stays, sustains,
spreads his wings and flies against the wind
why are you flying against the wind?

Black Air

Oh Death,
your sting is getting dull.

Oh Peace,
can you hear my call?

Oh Mercy,
you're far too strong
for me.

I'm weak.

Cause all I breathe
is black air
and I don't care
for saving
and I don't care
for the light.

Oh Lord,
Can you hear me now?

How can you go on
without a sound?
All I see
is the black air around me.

Oh Lord,
if you're saving me
come save me now.

Cause all I breathe
is black air
and I don't care
for saving
and I don't care
for the light.

Big Sister

To all my little brothers and sisters
who put me on a pedestal,
I have a secret I've never dared to share,
for my purpose was to make space
for all of who you are
and love every inch of you.
But let me tell you
that purpose made my life worth living
when I longed to ascend up
up, up, into the tearless clouds
where suffering is no more,
perhaps all is no more,
where peace abounds
and rest is found
in the chorus of angels singing the lullaby of eternity.
When I longed to escape out,
out, away from the utter darkness
where corruption resounds
where dreams lose their fervour
and humanity disappoints.
When this rock felt like a prison,
you were the humanity I clung to.
So no matter how much you thank me
for whatever I did
I will always be more thankful to you
for letting me in,

for letting Love flow.

It was better than heaven.

It was heaven.

The Royal Mountain

Petals on the trees
Branches of beauty

Fooled by the promises of peace

The garden fell
Into the valley

Forsaken in the Shadow of the King

The darkness reigns down
The clouds call out

The Snakes gather around
Stones rising from the ground

A wall grows and blackens your crown

Then the serpent turns to sword
And the stones become a road

A friend begins to take the wall down

Brick by brick

Brick by brick

Brick by brick

His love rings out:

"Hear my voice

Trust my words

I am known

I am Known

In your heart

In your mind

In your soul

and in your arms

Know that I am

for you now"

"And I will wait
for you to let
me lead the way back home.
And if it takes
a thousand years

You are where I belong

Whichever mountainside you're on."

The Anointed One

"I truly believe you are going to change the world."
That's what they said when I was fifteen.
I was told I was anointed,
and I believed them.

I preached my first sermon at sixteen.
A pastor said they couldn't have preached a better sermon if
        they tried.
I was told I was anointed,
and I believed them.

I led my first song in worship at seventeen.
A church leader said they hadn't worshipped like that in over
        ten years.
I was told I was anointed,
and I believed them.

I was hired for my first job in ministry at eighteen,
flown across the country.
I was told I was anointed,
and I believed them.

I travelled,
leading in some of the most successful churches in the world.
St. Catharines, Vancouver, Toronto, London, Montreal.

I interpreted dreams, performed miracles, spoke in the tongue of
        angels.

"You changed my life," they said.
And I believed them.

I made it.
At 23 years old.
At 23 years old,
I lost it.

I said that being gay is not a sin
and they took back my anointing.
I said that other religions aren't demonic
and they took back my wings.
I said that hell isn't real
and they took back my faith.

I studied hermeneutics and eschatology,
Christology and historical theology.
I learned a language that no longer exists
just so I could read the original, sacred texts
and discover the true meaning of mystery.

Still, they told me I was straying,
for I had questions
and I chased them down with all of my
heart, and

mind, and
soul.

What if I *was* straying?
What if I was straying away from religious violence?
Shouldn't we all?
I thought I was anointed?

"You're just hurt," they said.
And I was.
I've always been.
We all are.

And the truth is,
I wasn't really anointed.
I just had a tender heart,
and a bright flame,
and a reckless abandon.

And they loved it
until they could no longer control it.

Bear Fighter

Animals can smell fear.
They can sense it in your voice,
your body,
your breath.
That's why screaming at a black bear might not work.

Every summer my family would go camping.
We would usually see some
crossing the road,
roaming through campsites,
rummaging through the trash,
climbing the trees.

They were harmless,
but they were also wild.
So we followed the rules:
If there's a cub,
get as far away as possible.
If one does approach you,
make yourself big
and loud
and scary.

So when the largest black bear I've ever seen,

it's face covered in scars,
over seven feet tall,
thought he would have my dog for dinner
and threatened my friend who stood petrified between them,
I knew exactly what I needed to do.

My great, great grandfather,
Pépé Patry,
he had blueberry bushes at his cottage
and every morning he would sit on his yellow rocking chair on
         the porch
to watch the black bears eat the blueberries.

I've passed by bears.
I've protected cubs from reckless humans.
I've had a young bear visit me in the middle of the afternoon
         while I was reading by a warm fire.

I've charged a bear,
with the roar of a lion,
and the conviction of a bull,
and sent it on its way.

I'll tell you the truth:
I'm not actually a bear fighter.
I'm a bear whisperer.

Passerby

Flying over nowhere
on my way to somewhere.
Looking out the window,
my eyes adjust so I can see
the neverending stars
and faint clouds below me.

There's just so much space.
Empty space
over endless waters.
And I'm so small,
just passing through for a moment.

There's so much more than this—
more than I can fathom.
Today, of all days, something is reawakening in me.
Something I've forced away in pain.
Something that betrayed me and left me with nothing but
            questions.
Faith… Truth… God…
After years of being half-imprisoned by my own hands,
and surviving off the binges of other people's thoughts,
my own are finally taking form—
unlocking the rusty, cell door to my spirit,

burst open by the suicidal attempt to catch the light.

As a child, I wanted to know everything.
I was tortured with what my future could be.
I know now, it is what it is.
I am who I Am.
It's a mystery that troubles me no more.
I've found joy in a new mystery.
The blue flower, that mystical truth,
glimpsed only through stories, questions, art, and love lived.
A mystery not to be answered,
but enjoyed.
An insufferable joy,
always teasing me.

Will there always be something I'm missing?
I can feel the allure of the occult—*hidden knowledge*.
But that's just not life, is it?
It's not simple.
Nor is it hidden.
It's staring us in the face,
with eyes too big to recognize.
It seems to us a vast empty space,
and we're just passing through
only for a moment.

Disabled

What makes you feel good?
What makes you tick?
What fuels your soul
so that you need it?

You wish you could settle.
You wish you could focus.
You wish you could just do
what pays the tax of living.

But you can't.
And you deplete like an old phone battery
just trying to work sixty hours a week
to survive.

Either I'm disabled
or late-stage capitalism is gaslighting an entire generation.
Or both.

I don't choose to have a stubborn brain,
for the pragmatism of having a dopamine depletion is
lethal to a labourer in this capital C economy.

ADHD is a disability.
It's in the powerlessness of not being able to do a simple task.
Of not being able to tell the time,
not being able to remember,
remember, just remember,
God dammit, remember!
Anything.
No matter how important or life threatening.

It's always being concerned with having early-onset dementia.
It's in the agony of figuring out how to function just in time to
          find your body shutting down from over-exertion.
It's in the hair falling out in clumps,
weight loss and floating poop,
hypersalivation and fungus on your lips,
chronic back pain and pinched nerves.
Did you know ADHD brains need more sleep?
Is that really a surprise?

ADHD is a disability,
and the only thing that works
is doing what you love
and hope it loves you back.
At least, enough to pay the bills.
And eventually, with help, it does work

for those of us who last long enough.[1]

---

1   One in four women with ADHD have attempted suicide. "The Dark Side of ADHD: Factors Associated With Suicide Attempts Among Those With ADHD in a National Representative Canadian Sample " by Esme Fuller-Thomson, Raphaël Nahar Rivière, Lauren Carrique, and Senyo Agbeyaka Archives of Suicide Research.

Wanderer

The smell of Paris in the morning is fresh bread.
I'm strolling through a kitchen with one hundred ovens,
each with dozens of baguettes and pain de campagne and
        croissants
rising with me on this rainy morning.
The patisseries have already been bustling for hours.
It's 5:00am.

The second smell is cheese.
Pungent, dominant, almost sexual.
Trucks are emptying their crates at the fromageries
as I pass by them in a cheese euphoria.

The third smell is rain,
a scent that's familiar,
but it captures me in a new way.

Walking towards La Champ du Mars, I see the top of the Eiffel
        Tower.
It's not sparkling with lights as I expected, but draped in shadow,
a black silhouette against a dark sky.
It seems I've awoken before her.

The first sound I hear is the singing of the birds and faint traffic,
then the rhythmic footsteps of a dedicated jogger.

The park is empty, a stark contrast to the crowds yesterday.
I sit on a bench and open my notebook.
As I begin writing about the smells and sounds of Paris at 5am,
I realize I'm not alone.
Someone is watching me.
I hear them scuttle across the wet, fallen leaves.

    Could it be?

      Alone in front of the towering lady,

        Remy and I meet at last.

Dreamer

Sitting in the Bird and Baby, reading
Doctor Faustus in the place where
literary giants sat and drank and
thought, I'm reminded that C.S.
Lewis was a young person once,
like me, reading this literary
classic for the first time.

Instead of thinking about how different
my world is to his, on a more foundational
level, where things really matter, where
passion and ideas are innocently inspired
for the first time, we have much in common.
Wondering at the little things in life and
contemplating the larger, like how one simple
pub in Oxford that has stood through time,
people, wars, and depressions, students turning
into fellows and ideas turning into books,
can still pour a good drink that hits the spot.

Buzzed

My sister brought me an oat chai latte from Starbucks as I was
        shaving my head with my brother's old clippers.

She thought I was having a mental crisis.
Not an unfair assumption, to be fair.
We were in highschool in 2007
when a woman shaving her head became a symbol of hysteria.

I was shaving the finishing touches,
doing my best to clip the little stray hairs on my scalp,
when my sister-in-law entered with another oat chai latte from
        Starbucks.
This is when I learned that Starbucks is a love language in my
        family.

Emily also thought I was having a mental breakdown.
And I was
in the way I was breaking down my fear,
in the way I was breaking down my doubts,
in the way I was breaking down the rules of gender.

I've never felt so beautiful
as when I broke down my beauty.

The one who loved him

One day, my cat was struggling to breathe.

His name was Albus.
He was white.
My first pet who was my own.

He was saved from Texas,
a kill state,
and sent all the way to Canada,
where we met.

He had spent his one year of life in a cage
until I took him home.
After one month of being loved and kissed and cuddled,
he started coughing,
and then one night, he struggled to breathe.
I took him to the vet and they said he was dying and should be
          euthanized.
I cried.
I held him as they put the needle in his little body.
I held him as he stopped breathing.
I had never known what it was to be catatonic
until that afternoon when I went home empty handed.
I had never known what it was to be crippled with grief.

I buried him in the garden and I asked God:

Why would you give me a cat that would just die?
Why would you put me through this?

Immediately I heard an answer, deep in my soul.

A voice that was not my own said:

So that he could know love...

If a god exists, I think they care.
I think they feel pain.
I think they suffer with us—
even with the little, innocent animals,
so much so that sometimes
a cat who has never known love
may experience a love so true
in the last days of its life
at the expense of one woman's grief,
reminding her
that tis better to have loved and lost
than for a cat to have never been loved at all.

Collateral Damage

You're not the hero
You're not the villain
You're just the trampled grass beneath them
Waiting and hoping
For the hero to save himself.

Eastern Métis

Canada came for the half-breeds
who hid themselves as Français

Canada came for the half-breeds
who refused to assimilate

Canada came for their children
teaching them self-hate

Canada came for the half-breeds
and all those who'd migrate

Canada came for the rebels
who refused to fall in line

Canada came for the half-breeds
teaching them self-genocide

Baptized by snow

St Theresa of Avila blessed us among the birch trees,
shining yellow rays through the evergreen.
Grieving loss, celebrating life,
honouring love.

The forest was quiet,
filled with the presence of loved ones,
where the infinite meets the finite.
I sat on a log, closed my eyes,
and removed my toque in respect of the trees and memories.

I took deep, cold breaths,
as tears washed my spirit clean
and my Aunt Elspeth sang.

Then Elspeth made her intercession
reciting Saint Theresa as she took a fistful of snow
and rubbed it in my hair.

I became like that small child returning home
from an afternoon of tobogganing,
hair wet and frozen and powdered with snowflakes.

I was reborn in the snow.

In ye olde pub in the morn

It smells like two hundred year old wood
coated in a thousand layers of
tobacco, oil, and vinegar.
It never feels clean,
but you wipe it every morning just the same.

What's old is never really clean.
Things carry the memory of everything that's touched them.
You can repaint and reupholster and refurbish
but the smell never goes away.

You carry it with you,
with all the hope
and dreams
and disappointment it holds.

You carry it with you
because it's a part of you now.

Villager

It takes a village to raise a child
so as to keep them from feeling alone in life

It takes a village to raise a mother
so as to keep her from being overcome by life

It takes a village to raise a father
so as to keep him from being consumed by life

It takes a village to raise a family
so as to keep them from being lost in life

It takes a village to raise eachother
so as to keep us from missing life

Home

Maybe I don't know the truth

And I don't know what to do

I just know I'm safe here with you

I'm not searching for wealth or fame

Just a place that calls my name

And my heart will cry out

Hallelujah

Lover

To ask why I love you
is to ask why the moon
reflects the light of the sun,
why the tide moves in waves,
why water carves stone,
and coasts transform.

To ask why I love you
is to ask why messiahs die
and come back to life.

To ask why I love you is to ask
why you sweat when you're excited,
why things happen when you write it,
when you're attacked, why you fight it.

To ask why I love you
is to ask why fire burns
and cats purr
and the world turns.

How can I not?

Mummy

Your whole being
Lies heavy on my chest
It's as though souls have a weight to them
Your purrs rumble the melody
That unlocks my soul
Your head so small
Eyes so big
Claws so sharp
As they will me to stay
So I stay
Or I break away in pain
Or to my sadness and relief
You go on your way

The Virgin and the Whore

I am the virgin *and* the whore
The mother *and* the hag
The Madam *and* the spinster
The boxes which the patriarchy
Fashioned for my womanhood
I fill them all
And more

I am the virgin *and* the whore
The temptress *and* the nurse
The angel *and* the demon
I am also the hero *and* the traitor
The priest *and* the heretic
The explorer *and* the hermit

If you are to place me in a box
Don't forget all my boxes
There are too many to count
So it might take you some time
But this mission of placing women in boxes
is of your own choosing

So don't forget, I am the genius *and* the novice
The lover *and* the fighter

The reader *and* the writer
The warrior *and* the monk

I am the abuser *and* the victim
I am the captive *and* the captor
The rescued *and* the rescuer
I am the oracle *and* the seeker of truth
I am the box
and the space within
and the space without
I fill all them all
and more

But don't call me a mystery
I am not a puzzle for you to marvel at
I am who I am
As you are who you are
And we are all mysteries
For we are all human
And there is no limit to our complexities
So if I am mysteries
Don't sell yourself short
Of all the mysteries that you hold
For you too are the virgin *and* the whore

About the Author

B. C. Clare was born in St. Catharines, ON, Canada. Clare has published children's fiction, prose poetry, and essays of literary criticism and biblical criticism. Her topics include mental health, religious trauma, Christian mysticism, gender liberation, and decolonization. She currently lives in Oxford, England.

www.ingramcontent.com/pod-product-compliance
Lightning Source LLC
Chambersburg PA
CBHW050044040726
47599CB00015B/1793